PRAYERS
for
Young People

WITH READINGS FROM THE SCRIPTURES

by

ABIGAIL ACKER JOHNSON

PHILADELPHIA
THE WESTMINSTER PRESS

PRINTED IN THE UNITED STATES OF AMERICA

To Sam,

Abigail Acker and Harry,

Barry and David and Diane

CONTENTS

PRIVATE PRAYERS

[8]

INTRODUCTION

THESE PRAYERS, a larger number for individual use, and a smaller number for group use, are intended for those in their teens who often honestly admit, " I don't know what to say when I pray." Two years of teaching and living with young people have made me feel that a book might be written which would help them to get started. But the heritage of prayers that we have in *The Book of Common Prayer*, in the Forward Movement's collection of *Prayers New and Old*, and in such little volumes as John Baillie's *Diary of Private Prayer* should not be forgotten. While such prayers often seem too stiff to use at first, one should, even from the first, try to grow into them, and store up in memory some of these prayers and some of the psalms. Nor can any book of prayers substitute for our learning to open our hearts fearlessly, in our own words, to Him who knows our secrets, no matter how haltingly or unworthily words seem to come.

Passages of Scripture accompany the prayers in this book. It is to be hoped that these selections may help to open the riches of the Bible for those who still feel somewhat lost in it. It is also to be hoped that the connecting of Scripture with prayer will suggest that we cannot very well speak with God unless we listen to him.

Some of the private prayers have been written to refer either to a man or woman, boy or girl: the use of only the masculine pronoun has seemed to simplify reading of the prayers, but I should like to call attention to the fact that the feminine pronoun is to be substituted wherever necessary.

In writing these prayers, I have had particularly in mind the girls in my Bible Study Class at Sleighton Farm School, and the sharp questions they put to me. I am indebted to them, and to Mary Wood Daley, who made possible my hours with them. But I am indebted no less to my former teachers at Wellesley College, Louise Pettibone Smith and Paul Lehmann, for their suggestions and encouragement, and to Robert Francis Johnson, for his work with me on the revisions.

Abigail Acker Johnson.

Union Theological Seminary,
        February 1, 1947.

PRIVATE PRAYERS

IN THE BEGINNING *was the* Word, *and the* Word *was with God, and the* Word *was God. The same was in the beginning with God. All things were made by him; and without him was not any thing made that was made. In him was life; and the life was the light of men. And the light shineth in darkness; and the darkness comprehended it not. There was a man sent from God, whose name was John. The same came for a witness, to bear witness of the Light, that all men through him might believe. He was not that Light, but was sent to bear witness of that Light. That was the true Light, which lighteth every man that cometh into the world. He was in the world, and the world was made by him, and the world knew him not. He came unto his own, and his own received him not. But as many as received him, to them gave he power to become the sons of God, even to them that believe on his name: which were born, not of blood, nor of the will of the flesh, nor of the will of man, but of God. And the Word was made flesh, and dwelt among us, (and we beheld his glory, the glory as of the only begotten of the Father,) full of grace and truth.*

— John 1:1–14.

MORNING

DEAR GOD, with thee every morning is a good morning: apart from thee nothing is good. Don't let me hurry away into myself and into my doings this morning without asking thee to come with me and to be with me. Let me, then, come first of all to thee, quietly and patiently, for this minute. In thee there is no hurry unless it is that all thy children may use thy gift of time for serving thee. But help me now, for I can't even come to thee to start a new day without thy help. Help me by not letting me be too sure of myself. And then help me not to be too fearful of myself. Just let me give thanks to thee that thou rulest in thy world and that thou rulest in me. Rule in me and guide me in all the difficulties and in all the fun and happiness that this day may hold. May I be free from the bad habits I know in myself. Help me, by thy power working in me, to feel and act as I should toward all the people I will be with today. Please use me for thy purposes: my purposes only disappoint me. Help me all day to remember Jesus Christ, since in him thou givest me the freedom and strength that are not my own, but are enough to see me through.

"I will praise thee, O Lord, with my whole heart; . . . I will be glad and rejoice in thee."

Amen.

O GOD, *thou art my God; early will I seek thee: my soul thirsteth for thee, my flesh longeth for thee in a dry and thirsty land, where no water is; to see thy power and thy glory, so as I have seen thee in the sanctuary. Because thy lovingkindness is better than life, my lips shall praise thee. Thus will I bless thee while I live: I will lift up my hands in thy name. My soul shall be satisfied as with marrow and fatness; and my mouth shall praise thee with joyful lips: when I remember thee upon my bed, and meditate on thee in the night watches. Because thou hast been my help, therefore in the shadow of thy wings will I rejoice. My soul followeth hard after thee: thy right hand upholdeth me.*

— *Psalm* 63:1–8.

HEAVENLY FATHER, open my eyes, I pray, to see thee in the doings of today, to act as knowing I can never anywhere escape thy sight.

"I will bless the Lord at all times: his praise shall continually be in my mouth." God, grant that this day I may praise thee not only with my lips, but with my life. Through Jesus Christ. Amen.

Each new morning, Lord, is thine: help me to use it so. Amen.

Lord, come and be with me today, and by thy Holy Spirit guide me and protect me from temptation. In Jesus' name. Amen.

O LORD, *thou hast searched me, and known me. Thou knowest my downsitting and mine uprising, thou understandest my thought afar off. Thou compassest my path and my lying down, and art acquainted with all my ways. For there is not a word in my tongue, but, lo, O Lord, thou knowest it altogether. Thou hast beset me behind and before, and laid thine hand upon me. Such knowledge is too wonderful for me; it is high, I cannot attain unto it. Whither shall I go from thy spirit? or whither shall I flee from thy presence? If I ascend up into heaven, thou art there: if I make my bed in hell, behold, thou art there. If I take the wings of the morning, and dwell in the uttermost parts of the sea; even there shall thy hand lead me, and thy right hand shall hold me. If I say, Surely the darkness shall cover me; even the night shall be light about me. Yea, the darkness hideth not from thee; but the night shineth as the day: the darkness and the light are both alike to thee.*

— Psalm 139:1–12.

EVENING

DEAR HEAVENLY FATHER, now that the day is over, I need to talk it over with thee. Don't let me think I can hide any part of it from thee. Thou knowest where I fell down, and thou knowest the times when I just didn't listen to thee. Let me listen now, just to thee, so that thou mayest point out all the things I did that I ought not to have done . . . . . and those things I didn't do that I should have done . . . . . . And now please forgive me, for Jesus Christ's sake, since thou dost accept his obedience on the cross in place of my disobedience. Help me to be humble and thankful, to thank thee for using even my disobedience for bringing me back to trusting thee alone. Help me to thank thee too for whatever good was done through me today. Thanks for the high moments of gladness and happiness that thou hast given me through the people I have been with today, and through the things I have done to-day. I didn't deserve this happiness, and for such a gift, and for all thy gifts, I want to be truly thankful.

Don't let me pray only for myself tonight. Bless, I pray thee, all the members of my family and all my friends. Care for those children of thine whom I don't know, the world over, who are in great need of thy mercy and help tonight. Look lovingly on all who are in despair, in illness, in danger; free those who suffer at the hands of others; bless all those who struggle to serve thee.

And now let me really trust everything, all disappointments, all worries, all hopes, to thee for the night. Give me rest and strength for tomorrow and do in me whatever is thy will. In Jesus' name. Amen.

I WILL LIFT UP MINE EYES *unto the hills, from whence cometh my help. My help cometh from the Lord, which made heaven and earth. He will not suffer thy foot to be moved: he that keepeth thee will not slumber. Behold, he that keepeth Israel shall neither slumber nor sleep. The Lord is thy keeper: the Lord is thy shade upon thy right hand. The sun shall not smite thee by day, nor the moon by night. The Lord shall preserve thee from all evil: he shall preserve thy soul. The Lord shall preserve thy going out and thy coming in from this time forth, and even for evermore.*

— *Psalm* 121.

Loving Father, thou knowest the secrets and burdens of my heart tonight. Help me to hand them over to thee and just to take hold of thy forgiveness. Let me not heap one troubled day on top of another, but leave behind my vain reliance on myself, and give myself up to whatever may be thy will. " I will both lay me down in peace, and sleep: for thou, Lord, only makest me dwell in safety." Amen.

Heavenly Father, watch over me this night and grant that these hours of rest may make me strong to do thy will. Through Jesus Christ. Amen.

Unto thee, O Lord do I lift up my soul. Help me, Father, now, for this night, to give myself wholly over to thee, trusting to thy hands what will come out of the day that is past, and what tomorrow may bring, since the wisdom and the power and the glory are all thine forever. Amen.

AND HE CAME TO NAZARETH, *where he had been brought up: and, as his custom was, he went into the synagogue on the sabbath day, and stood up for to read. And there was delivered unto him the book of the prophet Esaias. And when he had opened the book, he found the place where it was written, The Spirit of the Lord is upon me, because he hath anointed me to preach the gospel to the poor; he hath sent me to heal the brokenhearted, to preach deliverance to the captives, and recovering of sight to the blind, to set at liberty them that are bruised, to preach the acceptable year of the Lord. And he closed the book, and he gave it again to the minister, and sat down. And the eyes of all them that were in the synagogue were fastened on him. And he began to say unto them, This day is this scripture fulfilled in your ears. And all bare him witness, and wondered at the gracious words which proceeded out of his mouth.*

— Luke 4:16–22a.

SUNDAY

DEAR FATHER, all days are thine and to be used in serving thee, but on this day especially set aside for worship, let me give special time to thee. Help me in the reading, in the resting, in the family gathering, and in whatever I do today, to see anew how thou workest in thy world. Let me find no excuse for staying away from Church. Help me to go in humble remembering that I am only one of thy children, that I live in the world full of thy children and need to worship with them. Give me ears that really hear what is told of thee in the Bible, since I cannot tell myself about thee who made me one of thy creatures. Speak to me, if thou wilt, in every part of the service, and keep my attention. And don't let me think it is good of me to go to Church, but let me be reminded that I am only one of thy wandering children, in great need of thee, and happy only when I dare to trust thee alone. Hear my prayer, for the sake of Jesus Christ, who was raised on this first day of the week to be the Lord of us all. Amen.

O GIVE THANKS UNTO THE LORD, *for he is good: for his mercy endureth for ever. Let the redeemed of the Lord say so, whom he hath redeemed from the hand of the enemy; and gathered them out of the lands, from the east, and from the west, from the north, and from the south. They wandered in the wilderness in a solitary way; they found no city to dwell in. Hungry and thirsty, their soul fainted in them. Then they cried unto the Lord in their trouble, and he delivered them out of their distresses. And he led them forth by the right way, that they might go to a city of habitation. Oh that men would praise the Lord for his goodness, and for his wonderful works to the children of men!*

For he satisfieth the longing soul, and filleth the hungry soul with goodness. Such as sit in darkness and in the shadow of death, being bound in affliction and iron; because they rebelled against the words of God, and contemned the counsel of the most High: therefore he brought down their heart with labour; they fell down, and there was none to help. Then they cried unto the Lord in their trouble, and he saved them out of their distresses. He brought them out of darkness and the shadow of death, and brake their bands in sunder. Oh that men would praise the Lord for his goodness, and for his wonderful works to the children of men!

— Psalm 107:1-15.

THANKSGIVING DAY

MOST MERCIFUL FATHER, help me to open my heart wide to thee today. For all the countless blessings I have not deserved but that thou hast showered on me; for my family; for dear friends; for all the opportunities for fun and happiness; for growing in body and mind and spirit; for the protection, the shelter, the warmth, the clothing, the food, that I take so for granted; for all these things help me to be really grateful. I thank thee for this land that I have been born into and for its riches and its possibilities. I thank thee specially for these things . . . . . and these people . . . . . that have lately made me happy. On this day make me humble and ashamed before the thought of all that I have in no way earned. Help me honestly to confess these wrong ways in which I have used thy gifts . . . . . Show me how little I have given in return. . . . . . And forgive me, not because I deserve even to be forgiven, but because I believe that thou forgivest me for Jesus' sake. Help me to thank thee above all for thy gift to the world of thy son Jesus Christ. May I begin again today to show my thankfulness by growing in love toward thee and in service to all those around me.

All glory be to thee, O Lord.   Amen.

AND IT CAME TO PASS *in those days, that there went out a decree from Caesar Augustus, that all the world should be taxed. (And this taxing was first made when Cyrenius was governor of Syria.) And all went to be taxed, every one into his own city. And Joseph also went up from Galilee, out of the city of Nazareth, into Judaea, unto the city of David, which is called Bethlehem; (because he was of the house and lineage of David:) to be taxed with Mary his espoused wife, being great with child. And so it was, that, while they were there, the days were accomplished that she should be delivered. And she brought forth her first-born son, and wrapped him in swaddling clothes, and laid him in a manger; because there was no room for them in the inn. And there were in the same country shepherds abiding in the field, keeping watch over their flock by night. And, lo, the angel of the Lord came upon them, and the glory of the Lord shone round about them: and they were sore afraid. And the angel said unto them, Fear not: for, behold, I bring you good tidings of great joy, which shall be to all people. For unto you is born this day in the city of David a Saviour, which is Christ the Lord. And this shall be a sign unto you; Ye shall find the babe wrapped in swaddling clothes, lying in a manger. And suddenly there was with the angel a multitude of the heavenly host praising God, and saying, Glory to God in the highest, and on earth peace, good will toward men.*

— Luke 2:1–14.

CHRISTMAS

Most loving Father of all men, I thank thee for the happiness of this season and specially for the happiness of this day. I thank thee for all the glad ways in which we remember the birth of Jesus Christ, for the songs, the gaiety, the gatherings of friends and family, for the gifts by which we remember thy great gift to all men. Keep me from forgetting, through all the doings of these days, why this Christmas day is set aside for happiness. Help me to wonder at thy mercy in giving a Saviour to us, who deserve only to be punished for our disobedience. Help me to think about what humiliation Jesus Christ suffered for my sake, from his birth in the manger to his death on the cross. Make me glad for the possibilities of life on earth that thou hast shown by coming into this earthly life through thy Son, our Lord. May I be humble and grateful enough to make room in my heart and life for him, since it is for his sake that thou art willing to take me in, now and always. In Jesus' name I pray.

Amen.

FOR THE LOVE OF CHRIST constraineth us; because we *thus judge, that if one died for all, then were all dead: and that he died for all, that they which live should not henceforth live unto themselves, but unto him which died for them, and rose again. Wherefore henceforth know we no man after the flesh: yea, though we have known Christ after the flesh, yet now henceforth know we him no more. Therefore if any man be in Christ, he is a new creature: old things are passed away; behold, all things are become new. And all things are of God, who hath reconciled us to himself by Jesus Christ, and hath given to us the ministry of reconciliation; to wit, that God was in Christ, reconciling the world unto himself, not imputing their trespasses unto them; and hath committed unto us the word of reconciliation. Now then we are ambassadors for Christ, as though God did beseech you by us: we pray you in Christ's stead, be ye reconciled to God. For he hath made him to be sin for us, who knew no sin; that we might be made the righteousness of God in him.*

— *II Corinthians* 5:14–21.

THE NEW YEAR

HEAVENLY FATHER, since thou art always turning us from the old to the new through thy promise to us of forgiveness and freedom through Jesus Christ, turn me and turn thy whole world today from the wrongs of the past to a new life. Help me to be truly thankful for all that the past year has brought me, for the friends . . . . . the experiences . . . . . for whatever I may have accomplished through thy help . . . . . for even the great difficulties and disappointments of the year that made me turn to worship thee instead of myself. In this New Year, let me see thee more and more as thou standest across my way, guiding me, guarding me, commanding me, and forbidding me. Make me really open my heart to thee so that thou mayest accomplish in me and through me whatever may be thy purpose for me. I pray that thou wilt guard and watch over all my family and friends, over this nation, and over thy whole world in this year to come. Forgive us all that is past, and grant that we may, from now on, serve and please thee in newness of life, to the glory of thy holy name. Through Jesus Christ our Lord.
                                                                    Amen.

THEN COMETH JESUS WITH THEM *unto a place called Gethsemane, and saith unto the disciples, Sit ye here, while I go and pray yonder. And he took with him Peter and the two sons of Zebedee, and began to be sorrowful and very heavy. Then saith he unto them, My soul is exceeding sorrowful, even unto death: tarry ye here, and watch with me. And he went a little farther, and fell on his face, and prayed, saying, O my Father, if it be possible, let this cup pass from me: nevertheless not as I will, but as thou wilt. And he cometh unto the disciples, and findeth them asleep, and saith unto Peter, What, could ye not watch with me one hour? Watch and pray, that ye enter not into temptation: the spirit indeed is willing, but the flesh is weak. He went away again the second time, and prayed, saying, O my Father, if this cup may not pass away from me, except I drink it, thy will be done. And he came and found them asleep again: for their eyes were heavy. And he left them, and went away again, and prayed the third time, saying the same words. Then cometh he to his disciples, and saith unto them, Sleep on now, and take your rest: behold, the hour is at hand, and the Son of man is betrayed into the hands of sinners. Rise, let us be going: behold, he is at hand that doth* betray me.

— *Matthew* 26:36–46.

GOOD FRIDAY

ALMIGHTY GOD, help me to understand the meaning of this day. Keep me in wonder before the mystery of Jesus Christ, who was God, winning the righteousness for men that they cannot win for themselves, and who was made man so that his death might be counted for all men. Help me to see today, in Jesus' obedience to death, how great thine act of sacrifice and love had to be in order to make a way back to thee for disobedient men. Make me more humble than I have ever been before to see the greatness of thy love in the cross: when I look at it, clear out of my heart, if thou wilt, every cobweb of pride or of holding back. Help me today to see how, in all my denials of Jesus, I join the world in putting him to trial, in beating and spitting on him, in crowning him with thorns, in nailing him on the cross and parting his garments . . . . . . Grant me today, again and anew, if thou wilt, the forgiveness Christ won for me and for all men by his complete obedience. Help me, from this day on, to take up my own cross and faithfully and gladly follow him.   Amen.

NOW WHEN JESUS WAS RISEN *early the first day of the week, he appeared first to Mary Magdalene, out of whom he had cast seven devils. And she went and told them that had been with him, as they mourned and wept. And they, when they had heard that he was alive, and had been seen of her, believed not.*

After that he appeared in another form unto two of them, as they walked, and went into the country. And they went and told it unto the residue: neither believed they them.

Afterward he appeared unto the eleven as they sat at meat, and upbraided them with their unbelief and hardness of heart, because they believed not them which had seen him after he was risen. And he said unto them, Go ye into all the world, and preach the gospel to every creature. He that believeth and is baptized shall be saved; but he that believeth not shall be damned. And these signs shall follow them that believe; In my name shall they cast out devils; they shall speak with new tongues; they shall take up serpents; and if they drink any deadly thing, it shall not hurt them; they shall lay hands on the sick, and they shall recover.

So then after the Lord had spoken unto them, he was received up into heaven, and sat on the right hand of God. And they went forth, and preached every where, the Lord working with them, and confirming the word with signs following. Amen.

— Mark 16:9–20.

EASTER

ALMIGHTY AND MOST MERCIFUL FATHER, fill me today with the wonder and joy that thy promises are indeed fulfilled in thine own mysterious way. If I, with Jesus' own friends, have doubted that he was the Saviour and have thought that he was dead, let me have this morning new daring faith to believe thou dost accept his victory for the victories I cannot win. Let me dare to believe it is thy purpose to raise me up, for Jesus' sake, through all the little deaths of everyday failures and disappointments, and out of the bodily death that stands at the end of life. Plant in my heart today the Easter promise and the Easter joy that what I cannot accomplish, thou dost accomplish in me, and for me, through Jesus Christ. Help me today and all the days of my life to put my whole trust in his power and to find him risen and alive at every turn.   Amen.

JESUS ANSWERED and said unto him, Verily, verily, I say unto thee, Except a man be born again, he cannot see the kingdom of God. Nicodemus saith unto him, How can a man be born when he is old? can he enter the second time into his mother's womb, and be born? Jesus answered, Verily, verily, I say unto thee, Except a man be born of water and of the Spirit, he cannot enter into the kingdom of God. That which is born of the flesh is flesh; and that which is born of the Spirit is spirit. Marvel not that I said unto thee, Ye must be born again. The wind bloweth where it listeth, and thou hearest the sound thereof, but canst not tell whence it cometh, and whither it goeth: so is every one that is born of the Spirit. Nicodemus answered and said unto him, How can these things be? Jesus answered and said unto him, Art thou a master of Israel, and knowest not these things? Verily, verily, I say unto thee, We speak that we do know, and testify that we have seen; and ye receive not our witness. If I have told you earthly things, and ye believe not, how shall ye believe, if I tell you of heavenly things?

— John 3:3–12.

BIRTHDAY

DEAR GOD, I thank thee for the year that is past, for all the riches of blessing that thou hast brought me in this past year, for all the signs and promises thou hast given me for all my years. I thank thee too for using my failures and disappointments and mistakes. Make me grow closer to thee through each failure and unhappiness: forgive me for every moment of trusting myself instead of thee: strengthen my faith in thy forgiveness. Help me to pray earnestly for the year to come and in the year to come that thou wilt grant me a clean heart, and renew a right spirit within me. As each new day comes may I live it through as thou wouldst have me live it, and, if thou wilt, stop me again and again from setting my own purposes against thine. Open new opportunities to me; increase my abilities; deepen my friendships; help me, in all I do, honestly to think of other people. Teach me not to be impatient, and not to fear as the years move; teach me to be content both to be and to do, at this present time, whatever is thy will right now. Bless my parents today for their care of me through the years; guide and direct them too in the years to come, and make me in some way a blessing to them. Through Jesus Christ our Lord. Amen.

THEN JOSEPH COULD NOT REFRAIN HIMSELF *before all them that stood by him; and he cried, Cause every man to go out from me. And there stood no man with him, while Joseph made himself known unto his brethren. And he wept aloud: and the Egyptians and the house of Pharaoh heard. And Joseph said unto his brethren, I am Joseph; doth my father yet live? And his brethren could not answer him; for they were troubled at his presence. And Joseph said unto his brethren, Come near to me, I pray you. And they came near. And he said, I am Joseph your brother, whom ye sold into Egypt. Now therefore be not grieved, nor angry with yourselves, that ye sold me hither: for God did send me before you to preserve life. For these two years hath the famine been in the land: and yet there are five years, in the which there shall neither be earing nor harvest. And God sent me before you to preserve you a posterity in the earth, and to save your lives by a great deliverance. So now it was not you that sent me hither, but God: and he hath made me a father to Pharaoh, and lord of all his house, and a ruler throughout all the land of Egypt.*

— Genesis 45:1–8.

FOR SOMEONE ELSE'S BIRTHDAY

HEAVENLY FATHER, please specially bless . . . . . today on this birthday. I thank thee for bringing . . . . . into the world and for making my life richer through knowing and being with this child of thine. Since thou hast thine own strange and wonderful ways of leading thy children in new paths, blessing them and making them a blessing to others, do thou guide . . . . . in this new year. Help him in all the needs of the days as may be best according to thine all-seeing, all-loving plan. Guard and strengthen him; in all difficulties, comfort and uphold him; bring him year by year into the blessings thou hast stored up for each one of thy children, and into the joy of loving and trusting thee. Through Jesus Christ our Lord. Amen.

CHILDREN, OBEY YOUR PARENTS *in the Lord: for this is right. Honour thy father and mother; which is the first commandment with promise; and that it may be well with thee, and thou mayest live long on the earth. And, ye fathers, provoke not your children to wrath: but bring them up in the nurture and admonition of the Lord. Servants, be obedient to them that are your masters according to the flesh, with fear and trembling, in singleness of your heart, as unto Christ; not with eyeservice, as menpleasers; but as the servants of Christ, doing the will of God from the heart; with good will doing service, as to the Lord, and not to men: knowing that whatsoever good thing any man doeth, the same shall he receive of the Lord, whether he be bond or free. And, ye masters, do the same things unto them, forbearing threatening: knowing that your Master also is in heaven; neither is there respect of persons with him.*

— *Ephesians* 6:1–9.

FOR PARENTS

HEAVENLY FATHER, I thank thee for my earthly parents whom thou hast given me, and to whom thou gavest me. Help me to show my thanks to thee by looking, every day, for ways in which I can show them my love. Whenever I am impatient with my parents and set what I think is right against what they think is right, help me to be sorry, and to ask their forgiveness. But grant that my parents may protect and guide me always as thou wouldst have them, so that in obeying them I may be always obeying thee. Whenever they are wrong in what they ask or do, turn their hearts and bring them to love and serve thee truly. Help them, and help me, so that I may truly honor my parents. May I learn to be thy child by being their child. Bless and guard my parents, I pray thee, with thy most loving care, and grant that I may be one of thy blessings to them. Through Jesus Christ our Lord. Amen.

IF THERE BE THEREFORE any consolation in Christ, if any comfort of love, if any fellowship of the Spirit, if any bowels and mercies, fulfil ye my joy, that ye be likeminded, having the same love, being of one accord, of one mind. Let nothing be done through strife or vainglory; but in lowliness of mind let each esteem other better than themselves. Look not every man on his own things, but every man also on the things of others. Let this mind be in you, which was also in Christ Jesus: who, being in the form of God, thought it not robbery to be equal with God: but made himself of no reputation, and took upon him the form of a servant, and was made in the likeness of men: and being found in fashion as a man, he humbled himself, and became obedient unto death, even the death of the cross. Wherefore God also hath highly exalted him, and given him a name which is above every name: that at the name of Jesus every knee should bow, of things in heaven, and things in earth, and things under the earth; and that every tongue should confess that Jesus Christ is Lord, to the glory of God the Father. Wherefore, my beloved, as ye have always obeyed, not as in my presence only, but now much more in my absence, work out your own salvation with fear and trembling. For it is God which worketh in you both to will and to do of his good pleasure.

— *Philippians* 2:1–13.

FOR FAMILY

FATHER OF OUR LORD JESUS CHRIST, bless my family, into which thou hast set me, with thy tenderest blessing. I thank thee for each one of them, for the things I have in common with each of them, and for the differences between us that make our life together even richer. I pray for each one of them, in his or her special need, as I name them now before thee . . . . . . Help me to put my care for them into thy hands, since thou knowest their needs far better than I, and since it is thou who canst fill all their needs. Be in the midst of our life together to bless us, and to make us indeed thy children and members of a greater heavenly family. Let us not be drawn apart from each other by impatience or selfishness or disagreement, and when there are any separations bring us together again through remembering that we are all equally dear to thee. Through Jesus Christ our Lord, I ask it. Amen.

I AM THE VINE, *ye are the branches: He that abideth in me, and I in him, the same bringeth forth much fruit: for without me ye can do nothing. Herein is my Father glorified, that ye bear much fruit; so shall ye be my disciples. As the Father hath loved me, so have I loved you: continue ye in my love. If ye keep my commandments, ye shall abide in my love; even as I have kept my Father's commandments and abide in his love. This is my commandment, That ye love one another, as I have loved you. Greater love hath no man than this, that a man lay down his life for his friends. Ye are my friends, if ye do whatsoever I command you. Henceforth I call you not servants; for the servant knoweth not what his lord doeth: but I have called you friends; for all things that I have heard of my Father I have made known unto you. Ye have not chosen me, but I have chosen you, and ordained you, that ye should go and bring forth fruit, and that your fruit should remain: that whatsoever ye shall ask of the Father in my name, he may give it you.*

— John 15:5,8–10, 12–16.

FOR A SPECIAL FRIEND

DEAR GOD, I thank thee for the rare and wonderful and great gift of this specially close friendship that makes my life rich. Bless my friend and bless me in the things we do together and in the things we bear together, and use each of us to help the other if it is thy will. I thank thee for giving me this friend now in my need, and I pray that thou wilt bless him with thy special mercy and guidance and protection and love. Make our friendship lasting, yet keep us from leaning on each other so much that we might turn from other friendships thou mayest provide. Grant especially that our friendship may never turn us from thee, who art the one true Friend. Through Jesus Christ our Lord.   Amen.

PAUL AND TIMOTHEUS, *the servants of Jesus Christ, to all the saints in Christ Jesus which are at Philippi, with the bishops and deacons: Grace be unto you, and peace, from God our Father, and from the Lord Jesus Christ. I thank my God upon every remembrance of you, always in every prayer of mine for you all making request with joy, for your fellowship in the gospel from the first day until now; being confident of this very thing, that he which hath begun a good work in you will perform it until the day of Jesus Christ: even as it is meet for me to think this of you all, because I have you in my heart; inasmuch as both in my bonds, and in the defence and confirmation of the gospel, ye all are partakers of my grace. For God is my record, how greatly I long after you all in the bowels of Jesus Christ. And this I pray, that your love may abound yet more and more in knowledge and in all judgment; that ye may approve things that are excellent; that ye may be sincere and without offence till the day of Christ; being filled with the fruits of righteousness, which are by Jesus Christ, unto the glory and praise of God.*

— *Philippians* 1:1–11.

FOR A FRIEND GONE AWAY

DEAR GOD, since it is thou who dost bless thine earthly children with the joy of friendships, bless me now too as I miss this friend who has gone away. As we had happiness and blessing in being together, give us new strength and friendship even in this separation. Prevent us from missing each other so much that we do not do whatever is thy will at the present time; keep us from being so dependent on each other that we are not simply dependent on thee. If it please thee, bring us together again, and grant that it may be our Lord Jesus Christ who binds us together as friends both when we are together and when we are apart. In his name I ask it. Amen.

Likewise the Spirit also helpeth our infirmities: for we know not what we should pray for as we ought: but the Spirit itself maketh intercession for us with groanings which cannot be uttered. And he that searcheth the hearts knoweth what is the mind of the Spirit, because he maketh intercession for the saints according to the will of God. And we know that all things work together for good to them that love God, to them who are the called according to his purpose. Who is he that condemneth? It is Christ that died, yea rather, that is risen again, who is even at the right hand of God, who also maketh intercession for us. Who shall separate us from the love of Christ? shall tribulation, or distress, or persecution, or famine, or nakedness, or peril, or sword? As it is written, For thy sake we are killed all the day long; we are accounted as sheep for the slaughter. Nay, in all these things we are more than conquerors through him that loved us. For I am persuaded, that neither death, nor life, nor angels, nor principalities, nor power, nor things present, nor things to come, nor height, nor depth, nor any other creature, shall be able to separate us from the love of God, which is in Christ Jesus our Lord.

— Romans 8:26–28, 34–39.

FOR SOMEONE ELSE IN TROUBLE

HEAVENLY FATHER, since thou knowest all the troubles and needs of all thy children, and since thou dost tell us in Jesus Christ to trust thy mercy and power at all times, please hear my prayer for . . . . . who is in trouble. Support him in thine almighty strength, and give him the help now to do whatever may be thy will in this difficulty. Give him the daring to trust thy power to bring thy children out of all dangers, and to believe that thou dost teach us all, through all our troubles, that nothing can separate us from thy love to us in Jesus Christ our Lord.   Amen.

AND I SAW A NEW HEAVEN *and a new earth: for the first heaven and the first earth were passed away; and there was no more sea. And I John saw the holy city, new Jerusalem, coming down from God out of heaven, prepared as a bride adorned for her husband. And I heard a great voice out of heaven saying, Behold, the tabernacle of God is with men, and he will dwell with them, and they shall be his people, and God himself shall be with them, and be their God. And God shall wipe away all tears from their eyes; and there shall be no more death, neither sorrow, nor crying, neither shall there be any more pain: for the former things are passed away. And he that sat upon the throne said, Behold, I make all things new. And he said unto me, Write: for these words are true and faithful. And he said unto me, It is done. I am Alpha and Omega, the beginning and the end. I will give unto him that is athirst of the fountain of the water of life freely.*

— Revelation 21:1–6.

FOR SOMEONE ELSE IN ILLNESS

DEAR GOD, please especially bless at this time . . . . . in his illness. Comfort and uphold him in his particular needs and weaknesses, and restore him, I pray thee. Bring him through this sickness, if it is thy will, to full strength, and fullness of life, and to joy in thy great power and love. Bless and comfort too, I pray, all those who are in distress about . . . . . 's illness, and in all the troubles of thy children, remind us of how thou hast healed our lives through our Saviour, Jesus Christ.

Amen.

BUT SOME MAN WILL SAY, *How are the dead raised up? and with what body do they come? Thou fool, that which thou sowest is not quickened, except it die: and that which thou sowest, thou sowest not that body that shall be, but bare grain, it may chance of wheat, or of some other grain: but God giveth it a body as it hath pleased him, and to every seed his own body. So also is the resurrection of the dead. It is sown in corruption; it is raised in incorruption: it is sown in dishonour; it is raised in glory: it is sown in weakness; it is raised in power: it is sown a natural body; it is raised a spiritual body. There is a natural body, and there is a spiritual body. For this corruptible must put on incorruption, and this mortal must put on immortality. So when this corruptible shall have put on incorruption, and this mortal shall have put on immortality, then shall be brought to pass the saying that is written, Death is swallowed up in victory. O death, where is thy sting? O grave, where is thy victory? The sting of death is sin; and the strength of sin is the law. But thanks be to God, which giveth us the victory through our Lord Jesus Christ.*

— *I Corinthians* 15:35–38,42–44,53–57.

WHEN SOMEONE HAS DIED

FATHER IN HEAVEN, both almighty and most merciful, help me, by thy Holy Spirit, to pray. Help me to trust that whether we live or whether we die we belong to thee, who hast made us and who carest for us. Help me to trust that thou canst make the death that has come to . . . . . into a new and fuller life with thee, according to thy promises. And because the rest of us who are left behind cannot see through the veil that hangs between this life and the next, and because we know how much we will miss . . . . . give us thy comfort and thy peace. I thank thee for . . . . . 's life and for all that thou hast been willing to do for us through his life. Help all who have known him, and specially those closest to him, to turn to thee in their sadness, and to live now in even greater trust in thee. Grant that we may continue to be blessed by all that has come to us through . . . . . and we may now look even more to thee to learn what thou wouldst accomplish in our own lives. Hear my prayer for Jesus' sake, by whose death and resurrection thou hast conquered death for us all. Amen.

Now when they saw *the boldness of Peter and John, and perceived that they were unlearned and ignorant men, they marvelled; and they took knowledge of them, that they had been with Jesus. And beholding the man which was healed standing with them, they could say nothing against it. But when they had commanded them to go aside out of the council, they conferred among themselves, saying, What shall we do to these men? for that indeed a notable miracle hath been done by them is manifest to all them that dwell in Jerusalem; and we cannot deny it. But that it spread no further among the people, let us straitly threaten them, that they speak henceforth to no man in this name. And they called them, and commanded them not to speak at all nor teach in the name of Jesus. But Peter and John answered and said unto them, Whether it be right in the sight of God to hearken unto you more than unto God, judge ye. For we cannot but speak the things which we have seen and heard. So when they had further threatened them, they let them go, finding nothing how they might punish them, because of the people: for all men glorified God for that which was done.*

— Acts 4:13–21.

FOR AN INSPIRING PERSON

DEAR GOD, I thank thee for the wonder of fine people who once in a while cross my path and fire my heart and mind. Especially at this time I am grateful for . . . . . who has given me a glimpse of how thou workest in thy world of men. I thank thee for this person whose actions and words have met my questioning and my need, and have given me that sense of encouragement and gratitude that brings me to my knees again. Help me offer myself to thy service again because I have been with this servant of thine. *Here am I, Lord; send me.* And if thou wilt, continue to bless . . . . ., and continue to use him as a way of calling many people to thee.

Amen.

AND THE LORD SAID UNTO MOSES, *Stretch out thine hand over the sea, that the waters may come again upon the Egyptians, upon their chariots, and upon their horsemen. And Moses stretched forth his hand over the sea, and the sea returned to his strength when the morning appeared; and the Egyptians fled against it; and the Lord overthrew the Egyptians in the midst of the sea. And the waters returned, and covered the chariots, and the horsemen, and all the host of Pharaoh that came into the sea after them; there remained not so much as one of them. But the children of Israel walked upon dry land in the midst of the sea; and the waters were a wall unto them on their right hand, and on their left. Thus the Lord saved Israel that day out of the hand of the Egyptians; and Israel saw the Egyptians dead upon the sea shore. And Israel saw that great work which the Lord did upon the Egyptians: and the people feared the Lord, and believed the Lord, and his servant Moses.*

Then sang Moses and the children of Israel this song unto the Lord, and spake, saying, I will sing unto the Lord, for he hath triumphed gloriously: the horse and his rider hath he thrown into the sea. The Lord is my strength and song, and he is become my salvation: he is my God, and I will prepare him an habitation; my father's God, and I will exalt him.

— Exodus 14:26 to 15:2.

AFTER AN EXCITING EXPERIENCE

LOVING FATHER, since it is thou who decidest what all the moments of life should hold, I want to come to thee with my thanks for the thrill and excitement of this experience. Help me to be glad and to grow in thy sight through the happiness of this moment. Help me to see in this happiness the sign of thy loving purpose for all my life. Grant that I may show my thanks to thee by coming more and more to trust and to look for thy will in every moment. Keep my faith steady in both exciting and trying times so that I may glorify thee not only with my lips, but with my life. Through Jesus Christ our Lord. Amen.

AND HANNAH PRAYED, *and said, My heart rejoiceth in the Lord, mine horn is exalted in the Lord: my mouth is enlarged over mine enemies; because I rejoice in thy salvation. There is none holy as the Lord: for there is none beside thee: neither is there any rock like our God. Talk no more so exceeding proudly; let not arrogancy come out of your mouth: for the Lord is a God of knowledge, and by him actions are weighed. The bows of the mighty men are broken, and they that stumbled are girded with strength. They that were full have hired out themselves for bread; and they that were hungry ceased: so that the barren hath born seven; and she that hath many children is waxed feeble. The Lord killeth, and maketh alive: he bringeth down to the grave, and bringeth up. The Lord maketh poor, and maketh rich: he bringeth low, and lifteth up. He raiseth up the poor out of the dust, and lifteth up the beggar from the dunghill, to set them among princes, and to make them inherit the throne of glory: for the pillars of the earth are the Lord's and he hath set the world upon them. He will keep the feet of his saints, and the wicked shall be silent in darkness; for by strength shall no man prevail. The adversaries of the Lord shall be broken to pieces; out of heaven shall he thunder upon them: the Lord shall judge the ends of the earth; and he shall give strength unto his king, and exalt the horn of his anointed.*

— I Samuel 2:1–10.

IN TIME OF GLADNESS

DEAR GOD, be with me to make me really glad in this time of gladness, so that I may grow in it and in love toward thee, and so that it can mean something lasting for me. Bless all those who have had a part in making this good time for me: use me in some way to bring gladness to them and to others too. Grant, I pray, that I may be more and more awake to the heights and depths, the wonder and joy that thou providest for thy children in so many different and unexpected ways, and grant that I may come to thee in humility and love and trust in both the moments of sorrow and the moments of gladness. Amen.

THERE REMAINETH THEREFORE *a rest to the people of God. For he that is entered into his rest, he also hath ceased from his own works, as God did from his. Let us labour therefore to enter into that rest, lest any man fall after the same example of unbelief. For the word of God is quick, and powerful, and sharper than any twoedged sword, piercing even to the dividing asunder of soul and spirit, and of the joints and marrow, and is a discerner of the thoughts and intents of the heart. Neither is there any creature that is not manifest in his sight: but all things are naked and opened unto the eyes of him with whom we have to do. Seeing then that we have a great high priest, that is passed into the heavens, Jesus the Son of God, let us hold fast our profession. For we have not an high priest which cannot be touched with the feeling of our infirmities; but was in all points tempted like as we are, yet without sin. Let us therefore come boldly unto the throne of grace, that we may obtain mercy, and find grace to help in time of need.*

— Hebrews 4:9–16.

IN A MOMENT OF DECIDING

GOD, OUR LOVING HEAVENLY FATHER, be very near to me to help me in this moment when I have to decide what to do. Help me to be quiet and patient now, to listen for thy will and thy command. Keep me from any secret decision of my own which I might think is thine. Don't let me consider myself or what I myself might gain, either now or later; but let me ask how I may truly serve my Lord Jesus Christ. . . . . . And if I can only decide with great fear and hesitation, give me thy blessing and give me faith in thy forgiveness. Let me not trust myself, but only trust that thou canst do and wilt do with me whatever is thy purpose. Into thy hands I commit my decision and what comes out of it, knowing that the power and the glory are all and only thine. Through Jesus Christ.   Amen.

HE THAT DWELLETH IN THE SECRET PLACE of the most High shall abide under the shadow of the Almighty. I will say of the Lord, He is my refuge and my fortress: my God; in him will I trust. Surely he shall deliver thee from the snare of the fowler, and from the noisome pestilence. He shall cover thee with his feathers, and under his wings shalt thou trust: his truth shall be thy shield and buckler. Thou shalt not be afraid for the terror by night; nor for the arrow that flieth by day; nor for the pestilence that walketh in darkness; nor for the destruction that wasteth at noonday. For he shall give his angels charge over thee, to keep thee in all thy ways. They shall bear thee up in their hands, lest thou dash thy foot against a stone.

— Psalm 91:1–6, 11, 12.

BEFORE A DIFFICULT EXPERIENCE

DEAR GOD, I'm afraid this is going to be very hard to go through and I'm not at all sure I know how I'm going to manage. Please support me and fill me with thine own strength, giving me that peace which passes all understanding. Give me, I pray, thy freedom, not confidence in myself, but sheer daring to believe that thou forgivest both weakness and wrongdoing. If I can have thy help and freedom and strength, I can go into this without being afraid. Help me believe that thou canst, and wilt do through me whatever is thy will.

" God is our refuge and strength, a very present help in trouble. Therefore will not we fear though the earth be removed, and though the mountains be carried into the midst of the sea . . . Be still, and know that I am God: . . . I will be exalted in the earth. The Lord of hosts is with us; the God of Jacob is our refuge." Amen.

FOR GOD, *who commanded the light to shine out of darkness, hath shined in our hearts, to give the light of the knowledge of the glory of God in the face of Jesus Christ. But we have this treasure in earthen vessels, that the excellency of the power may be of God, and not of us. We are troubled on every side, yet not distressed; we are perplexed, but not in despair; persecuted, but not forsaken; cast down, but not destroyed; always bearing about in the body the dying of the Lord Jesus, that the life also of Jesus might be made manifest in our body. For we which live are alway delivered unto death for Jesus' sake, that the life also of Jesus might be made manifest in our mortal flesh.*

— II Corinthians 4:6–11.

IN TIME OF DISAPPOINTMENT

HEAVENLY FATHER, help me now to bear this disappointment. Remind me that thou carest for the sorrows of thy children, and that I do not need to feel sorry for myself. Help me to use this moment to come again to thee, from whom I so often wander. "Lord, I cry unto thee: make haste unto me; give ear unto my voice, when I cry unto thee. . . . Attend unto my cry; for I am brought very low."

Help me to remember that thy purpose wins through all the heights and depths of life. If now I cannot see thy purpose clearly, help me just to cling to thee, waiting till thou mayest make it clear. So strengthen me in my weakness and need and disappointment that I may come to trust in thee alone. Help me to come honestly to see whatever responsibility I myself have had in this disappointment, and how I may have taken it wrongly, and help me believe that thou forgivest me, taking me back and raising me up through Jesus Christ my Lord. Amen.

AND AHAB TOLD JEZEBEL all that Elijah had done, and withal how he had slain all the prophets with the sword. Then Jezebel sent a messenger unto Elijah, saying, So let the gods do to me, and more also, if I make not thy life as the life of one of them by to morrow about this time. And when he saw that, he arose, and went for his life, and came to Beersheba, which belongeth to Judah, and left his servant there.

But he himself went a day's journey into the wilderness, and came and sat down under a juniper tree: and he requested for himself that he might die; and said, It is enough; now, O Lord, take away my life; for I am not better than my fathers. And as he lay and slept under a juniper tree, behold, then an angel touched him, and said unto him, Arise and eat. And he looked, and, behold, there was a cake baken on the coals, and a cruse of water at his head. And he did eat and drink, and laid him down again. And the angel of the Lord came again the second time, and touched him, and said, Arise and eat; because the journey is too great for thee. And he arose, and did eat and drink, and went in the strength of that meat forty days and forty nights unto Horeb the mount of God.

— *I Kings* 19:1–8.

IN A LOW MOMENT

DEAR HEAVENLY FATHER, I'm sorry I get so low sometimes. Be with me now to keep me from taking it out on myself and on others. Comfort me and restore me to thy presence, and to that peace that passes all understanding. Save me from thinking too much about myself. Forgive me for loving myself too much, and help me to love thee and then to love my neighbor for thy sake. Search out in me all the worries that I have been storing up. I want to open them up to thee now instead of pretending I can hide them or can do anything about them by myself. By thy Holy Spirit come into my heart and turn it to thee. Help me to accept from thee healthy rest, and happy and humble service for thy sake. Help me to use this moment and all the moments of my life to turn to thee and to grow in thy sight. Forgive me, cleanse my heart, and renew a right spirit within me.

" Why art thou cast down, O my soul? and why art thou disquieted within me? hope in God: for I shall yet praise him, who is the health of my countenance, and my God." Amen.

BLESSED IS THE MAN *that endureth temptation: for when he is tried, he shall receive the crown of life, which the Lord hath promised to them that love him. Let no man say when he is tempted, I am tempted of God: for God cannot be tempted with evil, neither tempteth he any man: but every man is tempted, when he is drawn away of his own lust, and enticed. Then when lust hath conceived, it bringeth forth sin: and sin, when it is finished, bringeth forth death. Do not err, my beloved brethren. Every good gift and every perfect gift is from above, and cometh down from the Father of lights, with whom is no variableness, neither shadow of turning. Of his own will begat he us with the word of truth, that we should be a kind of firstfruits of his creatures. Wherefore, my beloved brethren, let every man be swift to hear, slow to speak, slow to wrath: for the wrath of man worketh not the righteousness of God. Wherefore lay apart all filthiness and superfluity of naughtiness, and receive with meekness the engrafted word, which is able to save your souls.*

— *James* 1:12–21.

ABOUT A BAD HABIT

SEARCHER OF THE HEART and Tester of the conscience, thou to whom all hearts are open, all desires known, and from whom no secrets are hid, I know I have this bad habit of . . . . . . I know it is thy command that I should not be chained down by this habit, but that I should be free for full and happy service to thee in all things. Please help me through thy strength, for my strength is so weak: by thy strength let me more and more come to master the habit that has had such a hold on me. I know that if I truly want to get rid of this habit that thou wilt forgive me and help me. For Jesus Christ's sake I pray thee to forgive me for my failure up to now to break it. I know that I can't rule in myself, but help me know and trust that thou canst and wilt rule in me. Soften the hardness of my heart so that from now on I may really let thee be the Lord of my life. Open my will to thine, for Jesus Christ's sake, so that his goodness may take hold of my life. Amen.

But now thus saith the Lord that created thee, O Jacob, and he that formed thee, O Israel, Fear not: for I have redeemed thee, I have called thee by thy name; thou art mine. When thou passest through the waters, I will be with thee; and through the rivers, they shall not overflow thee: when thou walkest through the fire, thou shalt not be burned; neither shall the flame kindle upon thee. For I am the Lord thy God, the Holy One of Israel, thy Saviour: I gave Egypt for thy ransom, Ethiopia and Seba for thee. Since thou wast precious in my sight, thou hast been honourable, and I have loved thee: therefore will I give men for thee, and people for thy life. Fear not: for I am with thee: I will bring thy seed from the east, and gather thee from the west; I will say to the north, Give up; and to the south, Keep not back: bring my sons from far, and my daughters from the ends of the earth; even every one that is called by my name: for I have created him for my glory, I have formed him; yea, I have made him.

— Isaiah 43:1–7.

TURNING OVER A NEW LEAF

DEAR GOD, I want to try again to turn over a new leaf. I am truly ashamed of many things I have done and much of what I have been. I want to remember that for Jesus Christ's sake thou hast forgiven me, and that I may start afresh, free to do thy will. Help me not to ask that I may be perfect overnight: keep me humble. But keep me confident that thou holdest out thy hand in loving mercy whenever thy children turn, ashamed, to thee. Give me thy hand and lead me in a new life of trust and obedience and gratefulness to thee. I ask it for Jesus Christ's sake. Amen.

BE YE THEREFORE MERCIFUL, *as your Father also is merciful. Judge not, and ye shall not be judged: condemn not, and ye shall not be condemned: forgive, and ye shall be forgiven: give, and it shall be given unto you; good measure, pressed down, and shaken together, and running over, shall men give into your bosom. For with the same measure that ye mete withal it shall be measured to you again. And he spake a parable unto them, Can the blind lead the blind? shall they not both fall into the ditch? The disciple is not above his master: but every one that is perfect shall be as his master. And why beholdest thou the mote that is in thy brother's eye, but perceivest not the beam that is in thine own eye? Either how canst thou say to thy brother, Brother, let me pull out the mote that is in thine eye, when thou thyself beholdest not the beam that is in thine own eye? Thou hypocrite, cast out first the beam out of thine own eye, and then shalt thou see clearly to pull out the mote that is in thy brother's eye.*

— *Luke 6:36–42.*

FOR A DISAGREEABLE PERSON

DEAR GOD, please help me to pray for . . . . . whom I find difficult and disagreeable. Since I have not yet found the way to love him, let me pray for him because thou lovest each one of thy children equally, and thou lovest him too. Make me ashamed because I am so quick to be annoyed with him. Forgive my slowness to remember that we are equal in thy sight. And forgive me for daring to set myself above thee in judging him. Make me ashamed of supposing that I deserve thy love at all. Bless . . . . . and help me to pray for him without being proud of it: keep me humble over my own wrongs. When I am with . . . . . , rid me more and more of all my pride and let me serve thee by serving this person for thy sake. Through Jesus Christ, who is the Lord of us both. Amen.

YE HAVE HEARD THAT IT WAS SAID *by them of old time,*
Thou shalt not kill; and whosoever shall kill shall be
in danger of the judgment: but I say unto you, That
whosoever is angry with his brother without a cause
shall be in danger of the judgment: and whosoever
shall say to his brother, Raca, shall be in danger of the
council: but whosoever shall say, Thou fool, shall be
in danger of hell fire. Therefore if thou bring thy gift
to the altar, and there rememberest that thy brother
hath ought against thee; leave there thy gift before
the altar, and go thy way; first be reconciled to thy
brother, and then come and offer thy gift. Ye have
heard that it hath been said, Thou shalt love thy
neighbour, and hate thine enemy. But I say unto you,
Love your enemies, bless them that curse you, do
good to them that hate you, and pray for them which
despitefully use you, and persecute you; that ye may
be the children of your Father which is in heaven:
for he maketh his sun to rise on the evil and on the
good, and sendeth rain on the just and on the unjust.
Be ye therefore perfect, even as your Father which
is in heaven is perfect.

— *Matthew* 5:21–24,43–45,48.

AFTER A QUARREL

HEAVENLY FATHER, help me not to be angry even if I had a good reason to disagree with . . . . . . Clean this bitterness out of my heart, and make me ashamed to quarrel. Let me think, not about his wrong, but about my own. Since thy voice speaks to me not about what is good in me and what is wrong in others, but always about what is wrong in me, forgive me, for Jesus Christ's sake, for my own pride and thoughtlessness. Help me to be humbled in remembering that it is only great undeserved love from thee which forgives me and takes me back to thee. Then let me be so humbled and so grateful that I can only be at peace when I have forgiven the person with whom I have quarreled. Make me, leaving all love of myself behind, and full only of the wonder of thy love, ask . . . . . 's forgiveness. Work also, I pray thee, in . . . . . 's heart so that we may both forgive each other and learn to agree and go on together. Help me, by this experience, to be so sorry for my failures that I shall more and more conquer them, and so be found a faithful soldier and servant of my Lord Jesus Christ. Amen.

AND AS JESUS PASSED BY, *he saw a man which was blind from his birth. And his disciples asked him, saying, Master, who did sin, this man, or his parents, that he was born blind? Jesus answered, Neither hath this man sinned, nor his parents: but that the works of God should be made manifest in him. I must work the works of him that sent me, while it is day: the night cometh, when no man can work. As long as I am in the world, I am the light of the world. When he had thus spoken, he spat on the ground, and made clay in the spittle, and he anointed the eyes of the blind man with the clay, and said unto him, Go, wash in the pool of Siloam, (which is by interpretation, Sent.) He went his way therefore, and washed, and came seeing.*

The neighbours therefore, and they which before had seen him that he was blind, said, Is not this he that sat and begged? Some said, This is he: others said, He is like him: but he said, I am he. Therefore said they unto him, How were thine eyes opened? He answered and said, A man that is called Jesus made clay, and anointed mine eyes, and said unto me, Go to the pool of Siloam, and wash: and I went and washed, and I received sight.

— John 9:1–11.

AFTER A MISTAKE

FATHER IN HEAVEN, I am terribly sorry and fearful about this mistake I have made. Yet thou canst make all things work together for thy purpose of bringing us all to rely on thee. Hear me confess the thoughtlessness and carelessness and willfulness that went into this mistake . . . . . , and remind me of the wonder that for Jesus' sake I am forgiven and freed. Please let me cast all my fear on thee, and trust thee to bless and help all those who may be hurt or upset by what I have done. Let me, trusting thy strength, keep from failing thee again. May I give over the trouble now into thy hands, and if there comes any time or any way in which thou canst use me to straighten out the trouble I have caused, let me be quick and glad to hear thy voice.   Amen.

AND WHEN HE WAS GONE FORTH into the way, there came one running, and kneeled to him, and asked him, Good Master, what shall I do that I may inherit eternal life? And Jesus said unto him, Why callest thou me good? there is none good but one, that is, God. Thou knowest the commandments, Do not commit adultery, Do not kill, Do not steal, Do not bear false witness, Defraud not, Honour thy father and mother. And he answered and said unto him, Master, all these have I observed from my youth. Then Jesus beholding him loved him, and said unto him, One thing thou lackest: go thy way, sell whatsoever thou hast, and give to the poor, and thou shalt have treasure in heaven: and come, take up the cross, and follow me. And he was sad at that saying, and went away grieved: for he had great possessions.

And Jesus looked round about, and saith unto his disciples, How hardly shall they that have riches enter into the kingdom of God! And the disciples were astonished at his words. But Jesus answereth again, and saith unto them, Children, how hard is it for them that trust in riches to enter into the kingdom of God! It is easier for a camel to go through the eye of a needle, than for a rich man to enter into the kingdom of God. And they were astonished out of measure, saying among themselves, Who then can be saved? And Jesus looking upon them saith, With men it is impossible, but not with God: for with God all things are possible.

— Mark 10:17–27.

ABOUT SELF-CENTEREDNESS

DEAR GOD, save me, I pray, from myself, from thinking too much about myself, from acting so much with an eye on what I want and like. I do not find my happiness this way. I find only failure and disappointment. Forgive and set me free, for Jesus Christ's sake. Open my eyes and waken every ability thou hast given me so that I may use all the opportunities that thou art willing to open to me. Let me, instead of serving myself, serve thee by serving all those about me. Keep my prayer from becoming a new way of turning in on myself. Keep my service to others from becoming another secret way of serving myself. Stir up in me the courage just to trust thee and to let thee work in me in whatever ways thou wilt. In Jesus' name, I pray.   Amen.

FORASMUCH THEN as Christ hath suffered for us in the flesh, arm yourselves likewise with the same mind: for he that hath suffered in the flesh hath ceased from sin; that he no longer should live the rest of his time in the flesh to the lusts of men, but to the will of God. For the time past of our life may suffice us to have wrought the will of the Gentiles, when we walked in lasciviousness, lusts, excess of wine, revellings, banquetings, and abominable idolatries: wherein they think it strange that ye run not with them to the same excess of riot, speaking evil of you: who shall give account to him that is ready to judge the quick and the dead. For for this cause was the gospel preached also to them that are dead, that they might be judged according to men in the flesh, but live according to God in the spirit. But the end of all things is at hand: be ye therefore sober, and watch unto prayer. And above all things have fervent charity among yourselves: for charity shall cover the multitude of sins. Use hospitality one to another without grudging. As every man hath received the gift, even so minister the same one to another, as good stewards of the manifold grace of God.

— I Peter 4:1–10.

FOR THE WORLD OUTSIDE

GOD, PLEASE DON'T LET ME FORGET the world beyond my private world of coming and going. Help me to pray for the whole world of thy children, for the people across this broad land in all walks of life, in all their ways of serving thee. Help us in this country to carry humbly the responsibility of our wealth and youth. Bless the peoples of all other nations and their leaders. Guide those who try to solve the great problems of living together in the world. Help us to keep peace by seeing how we all stand before thee as our Judge, so that we will not set ourselves up to judge others. Bless all those everywhere who are in need; those who are helpless, aged, crippled; those who are ill; those in danger or temptation; those who are bowed down by the greed or thoughtlessness of others. Watch over all the little children of the world. Bless all who serve in thy name both here and in all distant places of the world. Make their work, and the work of all who serve thee in any way, sure and strong. And use me in any way thou choosest for thy service. Through Jesus Christ our Lord. Amen.

WE THEN THAT ARE STRONG ought to bear the infirmities of the weak, and not to please ourselves. Let every one of us please his neighbour for his good to edification. For even Christ pleased not himself; but, as it is written, The reproaches of them that reproached thee fell on me. For whatsoever things were written aforetime were written for our learning, that we through patience and comfort of the scriptures might have hope. Now the God of patience and consolation grant you to be likeminded one toward another according to Christ Jesus: that ye may with one mind and one mouth glorify God, even the Father of our Lord Jesus Christ. Wherefore receive ye one another, as Christ also received us to the glory of God.

— Romans 15:1–7.

FOR A BETTER WORLD

FATHER OF ALL MEN, hear my prayer that thy Kingdom may come soon. Heal the sores of the world and come to rule thy rebellious creatures. Guide the earthly rulers of the world into the way of peace and justice. Grant that all who struggle to serve thee may receive thy blessing. Close the divisions between groups and classes and races and make us one human family here, and one heavenly family hereafter. Give the Church a strong sense of its duty in the world. Make us really want to give ourselves to the righting of the wrongs of the world wherever we meet them. Use me, O Lord, not because I or any number of men can bring thy Kingdom, but because, when I am obedient and patient, thou dost work thy will in me and through me. All this I ask for Jesus Christ's sake. Amen.

WHEN THE SON OF MAN SHALL COME *in his glory, and all the holy angels with him, then shall he sit upon the throne of his glory: and before him shall be gathered all nations: and he shall separate them one from another, as a shepherd divideth his sheep from the goats: and he shall set the sheep on his right hand, but the goats on the left. Then shall the King say unto them on his right hand, Come, ye blessed of my Father, inherit the kingdom prepared for you from the foundation of the world: for I was an hungred, and ye gave me meat: I was thirsty, and ye gave me drink: I was a stranger, and ye took me in: naked, and ye clothed me: I was sick, and ye visited me: I was in prison, and ye came unto me. Then shall the righteous answer him, saying, Lord, when saw we thee an hungred, and fed thee? or thirsty, and gave thee drink? When saw we thee a stranger, and took thee in? or naked, and clothed thee? Or when saw we thee sick, or in prison, and came unto thee? And the King shall answer and say unto them, Verily I say unto you, Inasmuch as ye have done it unto one of the least of these my brethren, ye have done it unto me.*

— Matthew 25:31–40.

FOR THE NATIONS

FATHER OF ALL MEN everywhere, look mercifully upon all the nations of the world. Grant that the hearts of all men may be turned in love toward thee, so that we may be citizens of thy heavenly Kingdom as well as citizens in the countries upon earth. Keep us in every nation of the world from that pride and from that patriotism which forgets that Jesus Christ is our true King. Unite the peoples of the world across the boundary lines of nations into one family with Jesus Christ as their head. Turn the hearts of the nations that are strong and proud; raise up prophets to warn them against living only for themselves; move them to fill the needs of the peoples who are in want. Have mercy on the nations where there is hunger or danger or disease, and grant that my own conscience may be so troubled by their needs that I will not be at peace until I have taken some part in ministering to them. Guide the peoples everywhere that they may raise up leaders who will earnestly work for the well-being of all nations and for peace between all nations. May I be quick to understand other peoples' ways and needs, and may I use my own freedom of speech, my money, my time, and, when I can, the strength of my vote, to bring about some understanding between nations and some help for the needy nations. Use me, Lord, if thou wilt, and hear my prayer for Jesus Christ's sake.

Amen.

THEN PAUL STOOD IN THE MIDST of Mars' hill, and said, Ye men of Athens, I perceive that in all things ye are too superstitious. For as I passed by, and beheld your devotions, I found an altar with this inscription, TO THE UNKNOWN GOD. Whom therefore ye ignorantly worship, him declare I unto you. God that made the world and all things therein, seeing that he is Lord of heaven and earth, dwelleth not in temples made with hands; neither is worshipped with men's hands, as though he needed any thing, seeing he giveth to all life, and breath, and all things; and hath made of one blood all nations of men for to dwell on all the face of the earth, and hath determined the times before appointed, and the bounds of their habitation; that they should seek the Lord, if haply they might feel after him, and find him, though he be not far from every one of us: for in him we live, and move, and have our being; as certain also of your own poets have said, For we are also his offspring. Forasmuch then as we are the offspring of God, we ought not to think that the Godhead is like unto gold, or silver, or stone, graven by art and man's device. And the times of this ignorance God winked at; but now commandeth all men every where to repent: because he hath appointed a day, in the which he will judge the world in righteousness by that man whom he hath ordained; whereof he hath given assurance unto all men, in that he hath raised him from the dead.

— Acts 17:22–31.

FOR THE BROTHERHOOD OF ALL MEN

O Lord, who hast created all men according to thine own secret and wonderful purposes, making each one of us different so that each is an individual person dear in thine eyes, grant that we may all use our differences to serve thee. Work in my own heart till there is no false pride left in me. Let me be glad for the gifts thou hast entrusted to me, for my nationality, my race, and my religion, but only because I may use them in serving thee. Help me to remember, not just in my head but in my heart, that I am no dearer to thee than another person different from me. Help me to remember that each one of us alike is judged by thee for his wrongs, and forgiven by thee for Jesus Christ's sake. Forgive me for all the times I have forgotten this. Whenever I have a chance, help me to be a brother to someone who does not look, or speak, or act like me, so that I may really be a member of the family of those who follow Jesus as their Lord. Use me to break down the stupid and cruel walls of prejudice between races and groups and religions. Help me so to study, and think, that I may say true things and kind things, at the right time, and perhaps change someone else's mind and heart. Help me to be always on the side of those who are abused by others, to give my time and my money to help them, to act always as thine obedient and loving child. In Jesus' name I ask it.   Amen.

FOR THE BODY IS NOT ONE MEMBER, *but many. If the foot shall say, Because I am not the hand, I am not of the body; is it therefore not of the body? and if the ear shall say, Because I am not the eye, I am not of the body; is it therefore not of the body? If the whole body were an eye, where were the hearing? If the whole were hearing, where were the smelling? But now hath God set the members every one of them in the body, as it hath pleased him. And if they were all one member, where were the body? But now are they many members, yet but one body. And the eye cannot say unto the hand, I have no need of thee: nor again the head to the feet, I have no need of you. Nay, much more those members of the body, which seem to be more feeble, are necessary: and those members of the body, which we think to be less honourable, upon these we bestow more abundant honour; . . . to that part which lacked: that there should be no schism in the body; but that the members should have the same care one for another. And whether one member suffer, all the members suffer with it; or one member be honoured, all the members rejoice with it. Now ye are the body of Christ, and members in particular.*

— I Corinthians 12:14–27.

FOR WORKERS AND EMPLOYERS

ALMIGHTY GOD, who hast called us to serve thee in different ways, grant that everyone may truly serve thee no matter what position he holds or what job he does. Prevent those who have great possessions or great power from oppressing those who are weaker than themselves. Teach the powerful that there is no power or goodness except thine. Turn their hearts so that they will use their gifts in obedience to thee and in service to others. Have mercy on all laborers; bring about for them more comfort, and money enough for all their needs of body and spirit, so that they may work with joy and rest when their work is done. Help men to co-operate and to make just rules for peaceful work in industry and farming and trade. Strengthen the groups that are weak, and then guide them into the right use of the new power they gain. Guide my own heart and mind so that I will rightly decide which groups are the oppressed, and grant me courage to speak up for them and strength to work for them. Look mercifully on all groups of workers and employers and managers and turn all men from conflict to agreement and fairness. Grant this, O Lord, so that thou mayest find us waiting obediently for thee when thou bringest thy Kingdom. For Jesus Christ's sake.
Amen.

If there be among you *a poor man of one of thy brethren within any of thy gates in thy land which the Lord thy God giveth thee, thou shalt not harden thine heart, nor shut thine hand from thy poor brother: but thou shalt open thine hand wide unto him, and shalt surely lend him sufficient for his need, in that which he wanteth. Beware that there be not a thought in thy wicked heart, saying, The seventh year, the year of release, is at hand; and thine eye be evil against thy poor brother, and thou givest him nought; and he cry unto the Lord against thee, and it be sin unto thee. Thou shalt surely give him, and thine heart shall not be grieved when thou givest unto him: because that for this thing the Lord thy God shall bless thee in all thy works, and in all that thou puttest thine hand unto. For the poor shall never cease out of the land: therefore I command thee, saying, Thou shalt open thine hand wide unto thy brother, to thy poor, and to thy needy, in thy land.*

— *Deuteronomy* 15:7–11.

FOR THOSE IN NEED

ALMIGHTY GOD, by thy Holy Spirit, help me to open up my heart to thee for all who are in need. Look in mercy on the troubles of all those, in this country and across the whole world, who are poor . . . . . or crippled . . . . . or blind . . . . . or sick . . . . . or old and helpless . . . . . . Protect all little children, especially those who have no parents and those whose parents do not care for them as they should. Comfort the prisoners and grant that they may enter into new lives. Bring thy peace into every home that is saddened by death. Be the companion of all lonely people. Be the refuge of all those who are in any kind of despair. Strengthen those who are weary. Look on the needs of all thy children, Heavenly Father, and in thy great mercy, fill all their wants. Make me quick to see the needs of the people around me, in my own home, on my street, in my class at school, wherever I may be today. Use me as an instrument of thy goodness to serve wherever I can, out of love and gratitude to thee for all that thou hast given me. So help me to be a true disciple of Jesus Christ, my Lord. Amen.

THOU THEREFORE, MY SON, *be strong in the grace that is in Christ Jesus. And the things that thou hast heard of me among many witnesses, the same commit thou to faithful men, who shall be able to teach others also. Thou therefore endure hardness, as a good soldier of Jesus Christ. Consider what I say; and the Lord give thee understanding in all things. Study to shew thyself approved unto God, a workman that needeth not to be ashamed, rightly dividing the word of truth. But shun profane and vain babblings: for they will increase unto more ungodliness. Flee also youthful lusts: but follow righteousness, faith, charity, peace, with them that call on the Lord out of a pure heart. But foolish and unlearned questions avoid, knowing that they do gender strifes. And the servant of the Lord must not strive; but be gentle unto all men, apt to teach, patient, in meekness instructing those that oppose themselves; if God peradventure will give them repentance to the acknowledging of the truth; and that they may recover themselves out of the snare of the devil, who are taken captive by him at his will.*

— II Timothy 2:1–3,7,15,16,22–26.

FOR SCHOOL WORK

HEAVENLY FATHER, please help me to make use of my hours in school and my hours of study. When the work is easy, grant me the patience to learn everything from it that may be useful in those days ahead which only thou canst foresee. When the work is difficult, help me to do it patiently and thoroughly, remembering that thou wilt give me all the strength I need, day by day. Help me to remember that my abilities, my time, and these years in school are not my own possessions, to use as I please, but gifts from thee to be used for thy purposes, which I do not fully know. Let me trust thee as I spend these hours, so that I won't be fearful, but can give myself to thy will. Show me, every day, something new of how thou workest in thy world, and let me be quick to see how thou mayest be preparing me for thy service. In Jesus' name I pray. Amen.

THEN THE WORD OF THE LORD CAME *unto me, saying,
before I formed thee in the belly I knew thee; and
before thou camest forth out of the womb I sancti-
fied thee, and I ordained thee a prophet unto the
nations. Then said I, Ah, Lord God! behold, I cannot speak: for I am a child. But the Lord said unto
me, Say not, I am a child: for thou shalt go to all
that I shall send thee, and whatsoever I command
thee thou shalt speak. Be not afraid of their faces:
for I am with thee to deliver thee, saith the Lord.
Then the Lord put forth his hand, and touched my
mouth. And the Lord said unto me, Behold, I have
put my words in thy mouth. See, I have this day set
thee over the nations and over the kingdoms, to root
out, and to pull down, and to destroy, and to throw
down, to build, and to plant. Thou therefore gird up
thy loins, and arise, and speak unto them all that I
command thee: be not dismayed at their faces, lest
I confound thee before them. For, behold, I have
made thee this day a defenced city, and an iron pillar,
and brasen walls against the whole land, against the
kings of Judah, against the princes thereof, against
the priests thereof, and against the people of the
land. And they shall fight against thee; but they shall
not prevail against thee; for I am with thee, saith
the Lord, to deliver thee.*

— Jeremiah 1:4–10,17–19.

FOR WHAT I WANT TO BE AND DO

DEAR GOD, guide me, I pray, into what I really want to be and into what I really want to do. Help me to use the gift of every day to move toward thy purpose for me. Don't let me be content with what is easy or with what I would choose for myself. Remind me that I always defeat myself when I turn my back on thee. Grant that I may have each day the patience to accomplish what thou hast assigned for the day. Make me honest about myself and my abilities, not setting for myself either a larger or a smaller task than thou hast provided for me. Help me to remember that all thy children can serve thee in many different ways, and that it is thou who art the only judge of whether each has served in proportion to his or her ability. Grant that I may so trust in thy power and in thy purpose for me that I may give up all my own concern for myself, and just gladly do thy command as it comes to me. So make me fit to enter thy Kingdom, for Jesus Christ's sake.

Amen.

AND HE SAID UNTO HIS DISCIPLES, *Therefore I say unto you, Take no thought for your life, what ye shall eat; neither for the body, what ye shall put on. The life is more than meat, and the body is more than raiment. Consider the ravens: for they neither sow nor reap; which neither have storehouse nor barn; and God feedeth them: how much more are ye better than the fowls? And which of you with taking thought can add to his stature one cubit? If ye then be not able to do that thing which is least, why take ye thought for the rest? Consider the lilies how they grow: they toil not, they spin not; and yet I say unto you, that Solomon in all his glory was not arrayed like one of these. If then God so clothe the grass, which is to day in the field, and to morrow is cast into the oven; how much more will he clothe you, O ye of little faith? And seek not ye what ye shall eat, or what ye shall drink, neither be ye of doubtful mind. For all these things do the nations of the world seek after: and your Father knoweth that ye have need of these things. But rather seek ye the kingdom of God; and all these things shall be added unto you. Fear not, little flock; for it is your Father's good pleasure to give you the kingdom. Sell that ye have, and give alms; provide yourselves bags which wax not old, a treasure in the heavens that faileth not, where no thief approacheth, neither moth corrupteth. For where your treasure is, there will your heart be also.*
— Luke 12:22–34.

ABOUT BLESSINGS AND TREASURES

EVER LOVING FATHER, I thank thee for all the blessings and treasures thou hast set in my way. I thank thee for eyes to see and ears to hear what thou hast put into the world for men to enjoy and use for their strengthening and happiness. Help me to see always how fine and lovely things, the grace of trees and the songs of birds, the skill of art, the depths of music, and the power of writing, all point to the one Creator of all things. Open my eyes and ears more and more to find that the heavens declared thy glory. But keep me from loving the blessings and treasures in the world so much that I forget that all these things are gifts. Help me to love, above all, thee, who hast provided these things to bring me and all thy children to worship and serve thee. Through Jesus Christ. Amen.

THEN WAS JESUS LED UP OF THE SPIRIT *into the wilderness to be tempted of the devil. And when he had fasted forty days and forty nights, he was afterward an hungered. And when the tempter came to him, he said, If thou be the Son of God, command that these stones be made bread. But he answered and said, It is written, Man shall not live by bread alone, but by every word that proceedeth out of the mouth of God. Then the devil taketh him up into the holy city, and setteth him on a pinnacle of the temple, and saith unto him, if thou be the Son of God, cast thyself down: for it is written, He shall give his angels charge concerning thee: and in their hands they shall bear thee up, lest at any time thou dash thy foot against a stone. Jesus said unto him, It is written again, Thou shalt not tempt the Lord thy God. Again, the devil taketh him up into an exceeding high mountain, and sheweth him all the kingdoms of the world, and the glory of them; and saith unto him, All these things will I give thee, if thou wilt fall down and worship me. Then saith Jesus unto him, Get thee hence, Satan: for it is written, Thou shalt worship the Lord thy God, and him only shalt thou serve. Then the devil leaveth him, and, behold, angels came and ministered unto him.*

— Matthew 4:1–11.

ABOUT THE STRUGGLE OF TRYING TO BE A CHRISTIAN

FATHER OF OUR LORD JESUS CHRIST, help me, I pray, to be a Christian in all the things I think and say and do, and in all the ways I go. Keep my heart restless until it finds its rest in thee. Save me from thinking that I am good, or that I can accomplish anything in my own strength. If I ever think that I am better than other people, stand quickly across my way and humble me. But raise me from the little deaths of my failures, for Jesus Christ's sake. Let me live entirely by the power that comes to me through him. Turn my thinking and talking and doing away from myself, and let me, giving myself up to thee, become a tool in thy hands for thine own purpose, and a true disciple of Jesus Christ, my Lord. Amen.

GROUP PRAYERS

IN THE BEGINNING God created the heaven and the earth. And the earth was without form, and void; and darkness was upon the face of the deep. And the Spirit of God moved upon the face of the waters. And God said, Let there be light: and there was light. And God saw the light, that it was good: and God divided the light from the darkness. And God called the light Day, and the darkness he called Night. And the evening and the morning were the first day. And God said, Let there be lights in the firmament of the heaven to divide the day from the night; and let them be for signs, and for seasons, and for days, and years: and let them be for lights in the firmament of the heaven to give light upon the earth: and it was so. And God made two great lights; the greater light to rule the day, and the lesser light to rule the night: he made the stars also. And God set them in the firmament of the heaven to give light upon the earth, and to rule over the day and over the night, and to divide the light from the darkness: and God saw that it was good.

— *Genesis* 1:1–5,14–18.

MORNING

OUR HEAVENLY FATHER, wake us, we pray, to thy gift of a new day, and do not let us go until we have offered it back to thee. Give us thy word of freedom in our hearts so that we may not go in our own weakness but in thy strength, confident that what thou hast promised, thou art also able to perform. Let us work and play together today conscious that we never escape thine eye or thy protection. Help us to offer all that we do to thee. When we are in need of forgiveness, help us to take hold of the mercy thou hast offered us through Jesus Christ, and to forgive in turn. Bless us, and accomplish in us and through us this day, we pray thee, whatever may be thy will, and whatever may be for thy glory.

Amen.

AND WHEN THEY WERE COME TO THE PLACE, *which is called Calvary, there they crucified him, and the male-factors, one on the right hand, and the other on the left. Then said Jesus, Father, forgive them; for they know not what they do. And they parted his raiment, and cast lots. And the people stood behold-ing. And the rulers also with them derided him, say-ing, He saved others; let him save himself, if he be Christ, the chosen of God. And the soldiers also mocked him, coming to him, and offering him vine-gar, and saying, If thou be the king of the Jews, save thyself. And a superscription also was written over him in letters of Greek, and Latin, and Hebrew,* THIS IS THE KING OF THE JEWS. *And one of the malefactors which were hanged railed on him, saying, If thou be Christ, save thyself and us. But the other answering rebuked him, saying, Dost not thou fear God, seeing thou art in the same condem-nation? And we indeed justly; for we receive the due reward of our deeds: but this man hath done nothing amiss. And he said unto Jesus, Lord, remember me when thou comest into thy kingdom. And Jesus said unto him, Verily I say unto thee, To day shalt thou be with me in paradise. And it was about the sixth hour, and there was a darkness over all the earth until the ninth hour. And the sun was darkened, and the veil of the temple was rent in the midst. And when Jesus had cried with a loud voice, he said, Father, into thy hands I commend my spirit: and having said thus, he gave up the ghost.*

— Luke 23:33–46.

EVENING

MERCIFUL AND LOVING FATHER, we thank thee for this day that is past, for the happiness that thou hast put in our paths, for whatever obedience to thee we have been able to achieve, for the richness of friendships, and all thy special protection of this day. Claim and use whatever good we may have done through thy help, and forgive us, for Jesus Christ's sake, for all those things we have failed to do. Help us now to pray for all those who are dear to us who are not with us here: bless them and give them rest tonight. And bless all those whom we do not hold dear, and all those whom we do not know, the whole world over, since they are also children of thine. Watch over us through the hours of darkness. Grant that before we sleep we may give into thy hands all our worries, and trust to thy care all our needs. Refresh us through our sleep so that we may do, in thy strength, whatever tasks thou mayest set before us tomorrow. In Christ's name we pray.

Amen.

BELOVED, LET US LOVE one another: for love is of God; and every one that loveth is born of God, and knoweth God. He that loveth not knoweth not God; for God is love. In this was manifested the love of God toward us, because that God sent his only begotten Son into the world, that we might live through him. Herein is love, not that we loved God, but that he loved us, and sent his Son to be the propitiation for our sins. Beloved, if God so loved us, we ought also to love one another. And we have known and believed the love that God hath to us. God is love; and he that dwelleth in love dwelleth in God, and God in him. We love him, because he first loved us. If a man say, I love God, and hateth his brother, he is a liar: for he that loveth not his brother whom he hath seen, how can he love God whom he hath not seen? And this commandment have we from him, That he who loveth God love his brother also.

— I John 4:7–11,16,19–21.

FAMILY

HEAVENLY FATHER, bless, we pray thee, this family. In all that we do together may we help and strengthen each other and live together in that happiness which pleases thee. In the different things we do and in the different ways we go, keep us loyal to each other. Remind us that we are members of a larger family of all thy children and of all who try to serve thee. Work in us, by thy Holy Spirit, so that what we do together here may make us worthy to be members of that larger family. We thank thee for the fun that we have together, for the laughter, for the sharing of excitement or troubles. Forgive us for the moments when we lose our tempers, and for the times when we are not willing to give up something for the good of the whole family. For our failures and our selfishness, forgive us, for Jesus Christ's sake. Since thou hast first loved us, and hast shown us thy love in thy Son, our Lord Jesus Christ, help us to love thee in return, and to show our love to thee in our family life. Abide in us and among us, we pray thee, and grant that we may dwell in thee all the days of our lives and in the life to come. Amen.

IF YE LOVE ME, *keep my commandments. And I will pray the Father, and he shall give you another Comforter, that he may abide with you for ever; even the Spirit of truth; whom the world cannot receive, because it seeth him not, neither knoweth him: but ye know him; for he dwelleth with you, and shall be in you. I will not leave you comfortless: I will come to you. Yet a little while, and the world seeth me no more; but ye see me: because I live, ye shall live also. At that day ye shall know that I am in my Father, and ye in me, and I in you. He that hath my commandments, and keepeth them, he it is that loveth me: and he that loveth me shall be loved of my Father, and I will love him, and will manifest myself to him.*

— *John* 14:15–21.

FELLOWSHIP

OUR HEAVENLY FATHER, come and be among us by thy Holy Spirit so that we may really be bound together in fellowship. Bless our work and study and worship and all our doings. Help us to learn to live forgivingly with others by remembering that thou hast forgiven us through Jesus Christ our Lord. Grant that we may show our gratitude for thy love to us by being always ready to give ourselves up to thy service, and by seeking earnestly to follow our Lord and Master Jesus Christ.

Amen.

I THEREFORE, the prisoner of the Lord, beseech you that ye walk worthy of the vocation wherewith ye are called, with all lowliness and meekness, with longsuffering, forbearing one another in love; endeavouring to keep the unity of the Spirit in the bond of peace. There is one body, and one Spirit, even as ye are called in one hope of your calling; one Lord, one faith, one baptism, one God and Father of all, who is above all, and through all, and in you all. But unto every one of us is given grace according to the measure of the gift of Christ. And he gave some, apostles; and some, prophets; and some, evangelists; and some, pastors and teachers; for the perfecting of the saints, for the work of the ministry, for the edifying of the body of Christ: till we all come in the unity of the faith, and of the knowledge of the Son of God, unto a perfect man, unto the measure of the stature of the fulness of Christ: that we henceforth be no more children, tossed to and fro, and carried about with every wind of doctrine, by the sleight of men, and cunning craftiness, whereby they lie in wait to deceive; but speaking the truth in love, may grow up into him in all things, which is the head, even Christ: from whom the whole body fitly joined together and compacted by that which every joint supplieth, according to the effectual working in the measure of every part, maketh increase of the body unto the edifying of itself in love.

— *Ephesians* 4:1–7,11–16.

CHURCH

O GOD, bless, we pray thee, all people everywhere gathered together as the Church of Jesus Christ our Lord. Close up the divisions in the Church, and unite in love and peace all who call themselves Christians. Keep alive in thy Church its message, so that all men may learn of the victory over sin and death that Jesus Christ has won for us. Bind together in their faith all who hear and receive the Gospel. Draw us together by the power that comes to us through our baptism in Jesus' name, and through our remembrance of his Last Supper. Help us to join in humility and earnestness to carry out our duty in the world and fill the needs of men everywhere. May all who serve in thy Church, and all who hear thy word, work and wait in patience and in trust for the coming of thy Kingdom on earth. Grant that each one of us here may enter gladly into the fellowship of believers in thy Son, our Lord, and do whatever tasks in the Church thou mayest set before us. In Christ's name we pray. Amen.

SON OF MAN, *set thy face against Pharaoh king of Egypt, and prophesy against him, and against all Egypt: speak, and say, Thus saith the Lord God; Behold, I am against thee, Pharaoh king of Egypt, the great dragon that lieth in the midst of his rivers, which hath said, My river is mine own, and I have made it for myself. And the land of Egypt shall be desolate and waste; and they shall know that I am the Lord: because he hath said, The river is mine, and I have made it. Behold, therefore I am against thee, and against thy rivers, and I will make the land of Egypt utterly waste and desolate, from the tower of Syene even unto the border of Ethiopia. No foot of man shall pass through it, . . . neither shall it be inhabited forty years. And I will make the land of Egypt desolate in the midst of the countries that are desolate, and her cities among the cities that are laid waste shall be desolate forty years: and I will scatter the Egyptians among the nations, and will disperse them through the countries. Yet thus saith the Lord God; At the end of forty years will I gather the Egyptians from the people whither they were scattered: and I will bring again the captivity of Egypt, and will cause them to return into the land of Pathros, into the land of their habitation; and they shall be there a base kingdom. It shall be the basest of the kingdoms; neither shall it exalt itself any more above the nations; for I will diminish them, that they shall no more rule over the nations.*

— Ezekiel 29:2,3,9–15.

FOR THE NATIONS OF THE WORLD

ALMIGHTY FATHER, who art God over all the nations of the world, hear our prayer for the peoples of every country and for their leaders. Grant that peoples everywhere may choose for themselves wise and just rulers who will use their power only as a gift from thee. Be the guide of the leaders, so that they may lead their people into understanding of other peoples, and so that they may make and keep peace between all countries. Since thine is all the power and the glory, grant that the strong nations may acknowledge thy might and become humble and generous. Strengthen and heal the nations that are weak or divided or full of evils. Grant that wherever we may live or work, we may use all our opportunities and abilities to bring peace and justice into the kingdoms of this world, until thou shalt make them all the Kingdom of our Lord Jesus Christ.

Amen.

IF YE THEN BE RISEN *with Christ, seek those things which are above, where Christ sitteth on the right hand of God. Set your affection on things above, not on things on the earth. For ye are dead, and your life is hid with Christ in God. When Christ, who is our life, shall appear, then shall ye also appear with him in glory. But now ye also put off all these; anger, wrath, malice, blasphemy, filthy communication out of your mouth. Lie not one to another, seeing that ye have put off the old man with his deeds; and have put on the new man, which is renewed in knowledge after the image of him that created him: where there is neither Greek nor Jew, circumcision nor uncircumcision, Barbarian, Scythian, bond nor free: but Christ is all, and in all. Put on therefore, as the elect of God, holy and beloved, bowels of mercies, kindness, humbleness of mind, meekness, longsuffering; forbearing one another, and forgiving one another, if any man have a quarrel against any: even as Christ forgave you, so also do ye. And above all these things put on charity, which is the bond of perfectness. And let the peace of God rule in your hearts, to the which also ye are called in one body; and be ye thankful.*

— *Colossians* 3:1–4,8–15.

FOR BROTHERHOOD AMONG MEN

OUR HEAVENLY FATHER, who lovest us all though we are all sinners before thee, and who hast mercy on every one of us alike, through thy son Jesus Christ, grant that we may all live before thee as thy children and as brothers to each other. Turn the proud hearts of those who think they are better than some other person of a different race or nation or religion or class. Turn our own hearts so that we may always feel and speak and act as thou wouldst have us do toward a person different from us. Remind us that we have nothing to boast of before thee, nothing that is not simply a gift from thee to be used for thy service. Help us to use all our gifts to live with other men in this life as thy servants who hope to live in the Kingdom of our Lord and Saviour Jesus Christ. Amen.

FOR THUS SAITH THE LORD *unto the house of Israel,
Seek ye me, and ye shall live: . . . Ye who turn judgment to wormwood, and leave off righteousness in
the earth, seek him that maketh the seven stars and
Orion, and turneth the shadow of death into the
morning, and maketh the day dark with night: that
calleth for the waters of the sea, and poureth them
out upon the face of the earth: The Lord is his name:
that strengtheneth the spoiled against the strong, so
that the spoiled shall come against the fortress. They
hate him that rebuketh in the gate, and they abhor
him that speaketh uprightly. Forasmuch therefore as
your treading is upon the poor, and ye take from him
burdens of wheat: ye have built houses of hewn stone,
but ye shall not dwell in them; ye have planted pleas-
ant vineyards, but ye shall not drink wine of them.
For I know your manifold transgressions and your
mighty sins: they afflict the just, they take a bribe,
and they turn aside the poor in the gate from their
right. Seek good, and not evil, that ye may live: and
so the Lord, the God of hosts, shall be with you, as
ye have spoken. Hate the evil, and love the good, and
establish judgment in the gate: . . . But let judgment run down as waters, and righteousness as a
mighty stream.*

— Amos 5:4,7–12,14,15a,24.

FOR WORKERS AND EMPLOYERS

GOD, WHO ART ALL-POWERFUL, quiet the struggle for power between workers and their employers. May both those who labor and those who direct work do their tasks as servants of thine, who must render account to thee of their service to their fellow men. Strengthen all workers to meet the duties of the day with patience and responsibility. Bring all those who are strong to seek the well-being of all those who are weak. Grant that the workers may ask and gain a rightful time for play, sufficient wealth for all their needs, and all protection against sickness and danger. Bring about, between workers and those who own businesses and those who direct them, just and peaceful agreements. Help us to work in every way we can to see that all men may work with joy, and rest when their work is done, and live their lives as thy servants. Through Jesus Christ our Lord. Amen.

AND, BEHOLD, A CERTAIN LAWYER *stood up, and tempted him, saying, Master, what shall I do to inherit eternal life? He said unto him, What is written in the law? how readest thou? And he answering said, Thou shalt love the Lord thy God with all thy heart, and with all thy soul, and with all thy strength, and with all thy mind; and thy neighbour as thyself. And he said unto him, Thou hast answered right: this do, and thou shalt live. But he, willing to justify himself, said unto Jesus, And who is my neighbour? And Jesus answering said, A certain man went down from Jerusalem to Jericho, and fell among thieves, which stripped him of his raiment, and wounded him, and departed, leaving him half dead. And by chance there came down a certain priest that way: and when he saw him, he passed by on the other side. And likewise a Levite, when he was at the place, came and looked on him, and passed by on the other side. But a certain Samaritan, as he journeyed, came where he was: and . . . he had compassion on him, And . . . bound up his wounds, pouring in oil and wine, and set him on his own beast, and brought him to an inn, and took care of him. And on the morrow when he departed, he took out two pence, and gave them to the host, and said unto him, Take care of him; and whatsoever thou spendest more, when I come again, I will repay thee. Which now of these three, thinkest thou, was neighbour unto him that fell among the thieves? And he said, He that shewed mercy on him. Then said Jesus unto him, Go, and do thou likewise.*

— Luke 10:25-37.

FOR THOSE IN NEED

MOST MERCIFUL GOD, hear our prayer that thou wilt have mercy on all those who are in need. Bless the blind and the deaf and the dumb, the lame and all helpless people. Comfort the prisoners and give them hope of a new life. Give rest to the weary and food to the hungry. Come to the rescue of all who are worried because of the needs of body or mind or heart, and give them the peace of thy Holy Spirit. Specially we pray that thou wilt trouble our consciences and hearts about the needs of so many of thy children, and wilt give us no rest till we have ministered to them. Open our eyes to see the needs of those nearest to us. Grant that we may never pass them by, but that in serving them we may become worthy to be called followers of Jesus Christ our Lord. Amen.

LORD, THOU HAST BEEN OUR DWELLING PLACE *in all generations. Before the mountains were brought forth, or ever thou hadst formed the earth and the world, even from everlasting to everlasting, thou art God. Thou turnest man to destruction; and sayest, Return, ye children of men. For a thousand years in thy sight are but as yesterday when it is past, and as a watch in the night. So teach us to number our days, that we may apply our hearts unto wisdom. O satisfy us early with thy mercy; that we may rejoice and be glad all our days. Make us glad according to the days wherein thou hast afflicted us, and the years wherein we have seen evil. Let thy work appear unto thy servants, and thy glory unto their children. And let the beauty of the Lord our God be upon us: and establish thou the work of our hands upon us; yea, the work of our hands establish thou it.*

— Psalm 90:1–4,12,14–17.

SCHOOL

Lord, bless, we pray thee, our school: bless to thy service those who teach and those who learn. Make us grateful for thy gifts of learning that have come down to us through the years; help us to receive them rightly and to use them for thy glory. Inspire our teachers that they may be eager to teach, and inspire the students that they may be eager and grateful to learn. When we grow weary, remind us that thou dost not weary in strengthening us. Since we do not know what the future will require of us, help us to learn everything we can in the present: help us to give ourselves now to this present task so that we may be prepared for whatever tasks thou mayest provide ahead. Bless us in all our life together, and give us clean and humble hearts in all our doings. Grant, we pray, that as we live we may more faithfully remember thy gift of thy Son Jesus Christ, and, learning through him of thy great mercy toward us, may praise thee throughout all our days. Amen.

HAVE MERCY UPON ME, O God, *according to thy lovingkindness: according unto the multitude of thy tender mercies blot out my transgressions. Wash me throughly from mine iniquity, and cleanse me from my sin. For I acknowledge my transgressions: and my sin is ever before me. Against thee, thee only, have I sinned, and done this evil in thy sight: that thou mightest be justified when thou speakest, and be clear when thou judgest. Create in me a clean heart, O God; and renew a right spirit within me. Cast me not away from thy presence; and take not thy holy spirit from me. Restore unto me the joy of thy salvation; and uphold me with thy free spirit. Then will I teach transgressors thy ways; and sinners shall be converted unto thee. O Lord, open thou my lips; and my mouth shall shew forth thy praise. For thou desirest not sacrifice; else would I give it: thou delightest not in burnt offering. The sacrifices of God are a broken spirit: a broken and a contrite heart, O God, thou wilt not despise.*

— Psalm 51:1–4,10–13,15–17.

PENITENCE AND THANKSGIVING

OUR HEAVENLY FATHER, grant that we may all have penitent hearts as we draw near to thee. Recall to us how continuously we have been blessed with thy care, through family and friends, school and Church, and through all the many workers whom we too little remember, whose daily labor provides us with food and warmth and clothing and all our comforts. Remind us of how little we have deserved all thy mercies. For our undeserving, and for our misuse of thy gifts, for our forgetfulness and our failures, forgive us for Jesus Christ's sake. Make in us new and thankful hearts, that we may thank thee, not only with our lips but with our lives. Bind us close to all others who try to serve thee, and grant to us, and to them, the strength to do thy will. Through Jesus Christ our Lord. Amen.

WHEREFORE DAVID BLESSED THE LORD *before all the congregation: and David said, Blessed be thou, Lord God of Israel our father, for ever and ever. Thine, O Lord, is the greatness, and the power, and the glory, and the victory, and the majesty: for all that is in the heaven and in the earth is thine; thine is the kingdom, O Lord, and thou art exalted as head above all. Both riches and honour come of thee, and thou reignest over all; . . . and in thine hand it is to make great, and to give strength unto all. Now therefore, our God, we thank thee, and praise thy glorious name. But who am I, and what is my people, that we should be able to offer so willingly after this sort? for all things come of thee, and of thine own have we given thee. For we are strangers before thee, and sojourners, as were all our fathers: our days on the earth are as a shadow, and there is none abiding. O Lord our God, all this store that we have prepared to build thee an house for thine holy name cometh of thine hand, and is all thine own. And David said to all the congregation, Now bless the Lord your God. And all the congregation blessed the Lord God of their fathers.*

— *I Chronicles* 29:10–16,20ab.

THANKSGIVING DAY

ALMIGHTY AND MOST MERCIFUL FATHER, help us to thank thee most humbly on this day that is set aside for special thanksgiving. Recall to our minds and hearts all the riches of thy gifts to us, our young and wealthy country with its history of gallant men and women, our fine schools, our free Churches. Recall to our minds and hearts all the care and happiness and opportunities we have received through our families and in our friendships. Since we can in no way claim to have earned or provided these blessings for ourselves, and since they have come as free gifts from thy hand, give us a new sense of thy great love toward us. Help us now to confess our false pride and our neglect of thy gifts. Forgive us, we pray, for these and all our sins, and grant that our hearts may be more ready to thank thee and our hands more ready to serve thee, from this day on. Through Jesus Christ our Lord. Amen.

AND THERE SHALL COME FORTH *a rod out of the stem of Jesse, and a Branch shall grow out of his roots: and the spirit of the Lord shall rest upon him, the spirit of wisdom and understanding, the spirit of counsel and might, the spirit of knowledge and of the fear of the Lord; and shall make him of quick understanding in the fear of the Lord: and he shall not judge after the sight of his eyes, neither reprove after the hearing of his ears: but with righteousness shall he judge the poor, and reprove with equity for the meek of the earth: and he shall smite the earth with the rod of his mouth, and with the breath of his lips shall he slay the wicked. And righteousness shall be the girdle of his loins, and faithfulness the girdle of his reins. The wolf also shall dwell with the lamb, and the leopard shall lie down with the kid; and the calf and the young lion and the fatling together; and a little child shall lead them. And the cow and the bear shall feed; their young ones shall lie down together: and the lion shall eat straw like the ox. And the sucking child shall play on the hole of the asp, and the weaned child shall put his hand on the cockatrice' den. They shall not hurt nor destroy in all my holy mountain: for the earth shall be full of the knowledge of the Lord, as the waters cover the sea.*

— *Isaiah* 11:1–9.

CHRISTMAS

OUR HEAVENLY FATHER, who humbled thyself to come to us on earth, give us the true gladness of this day. Let us not forget that our rejoicing, our gifts, our gatherings, are in remembrance of thy gift to the world of thy Son Jesus Christ. Since there was no room for him in the inn, let each one of us give him all room this day in our hearts. Since thou wert content that he should be laid in a simple manger, may we kneel to him today as to our Lord and King. Since the wise, and the rich, and the poor, all had need of him, and brought to him what they had, may all thy children come to him today with whatever they can bring. Since thou hast had such mercy on the world that thou camest on earth, in this Child, to be our Saviour, let us, in awe and love and wonder, pray thee to forgive us and enter into our rebellious hearts. We need thee sorely, O God! Come and be our gladness on the birthday of thy Son, our Lord.   Amen.

AND WHEN EIGHT DAYS WERE ACCOMPLISHED for the circumcising of the child, his name was called JESUS, which was so named of the angel before he was conceived in the womb. And when the days of her purification according to the law of Moses were accomplished, they brought him to Jerusalem, to present him to the Lord; (as it is written in the law of the Lord, Every male that openeth the womb shall be called holy to the Lord;) and to offer a sacrifice according to that which is said in the law of the Lord, A pair of turtledoves, or two young pigeons. And, behold, there was a man in Jerusalem, whose name was Simeon; and the same man was just and devout, waiting for the consolation of Israel: and the Holy Ghost was upon him. And it was revealed unto him by the Holy Ghost, that he should not see death, before he had seen the Lord's Christ. And he came by the Spirit into the temple: and when the parents brought in the child Jesus, to do for him after the custom of the law, then took he him up in his arms, and blessed God, and said, Lord, now lettest thou thy servant depart in peace, according to thy word: for mine eyes have seen thy salvation, which thou hast prepared before the face of all people; a light to lighten the Gentiles, and the glory of thy people Israel.

— Luke 2:21–32.

THE NEW YEAR

WE GATHER TOGETHER to ask thy blessing on this New Year, our Heavenly Father. Help us to remember thy blessings and thy guidance and protection through the past year, the friends and the happy times, the ways in which we may have been able to grow, those things which, with thy Help, we may have been able to do to please thee. Help us, too, to remember those ways in which we have failed thee, those times when we refused thy guiding and protecting hand, those gifts and opportunities we used for our own ends, only to find that we were still restless. Forgive us for our past failures, for Jesus Christ's sake. Since we have seen thy salvation, may we put all our trust, our hopes and our fears for this New Year, into thy hands. Grant that this day we may commit ourselves anew to thy service and to whatever may be thy will for us in the year ahead. In Jesus, name.   Amen.

WHO HATH BELIEVED OUR REPORT? *and to whom is the arm of the Lord revealed? For he shall grow up before him as a tender plant, and as a root out of a dry ground: he hath no form nor comeliness; and when we shall see him, there is no beauty that we should desire him. He is despised and rejected of men; a man of sorrows, and acquainted with grief: and we hid as it were our faces from him; he was despised, and we esteemed him not. Surely he hath borne our griefs, and carried our sorrows: yet we did esteem him stricken, smitten of God, and afflicted. But he was wounded for our transgressions, he was bruised for our iniquities: the chastisement of our peace was upon him; and with his stripes we are healed. All we like sheep have gone astray; we have turned every one to his own way; and the Lord hath laid on him the inquity of us all. He was oppressed, and he was afflicted, yet he opened not his mouth: he is brought as a lamb to the slaughter, and as a sheep before her shearers is dumb, so he openeth not his mouth. He was taken from prison and from judgment: and who shall declare his generation? for he was cut off out of the land of the living: for the transgression of my people was he stricken. And he made his grave with the wicked, and with the rich in his death; because he had done no violence, neither was any deceit in his mouth.*

— Isaiah 53:1–9.

GOOD FRIDAY

ALMIGHTY AND MOST MERCIFUL FATHER, who on this day gavest thy Son Jesus Christ to death that we might live, make our hearts tremble to think of what thou hast done for us. Help us to see how the world and we, too, still refuse to recognize the Lord, and still put him to death, because we fear his power or want him to be for us something different from what thou hast willed. Humble us before his obedience, which thou hast mercifully accepted in place of the obedience we have not given thee. Keep us, we pray thee, from denying our Lord. Grant that we, forgiven through his death, may faithfully take up our own crosses, and find his yoke easy, and his burden light. In his name we pray. Amen.

BUT THOMAS, one of the twelve, called Didymus, was was not with them when Jesus came. The other disciples therefore said unto him, We have seen the Lord. But he said unto them, Except I shall see in his hands the print of the nails, and put my finger into the print of the nails, and thrust my hand into his side, I will not believe. And after eight days again his disciples were within, and Thomas with them: then came Jesus, the doors being shut, and stood in the midst, and said, Peace be unto you. Then saith he to Thomas, Reach hither thy finger, and behold my hands; and reach hither thy hand, and thrust it into my side: and be not faithless, but believing. And Thomas answered and said unto him, My Lord and my God. Jesus saith unto him, Thomas, because thou hast seen me, thou hast believed: blessed are they that have not seen, and yet have believed. And many other signs truly did Jesus in the presence of his disciples, which are not written in this book: but these are written, that ye might believe that Jesus is the Christ, the Son of God; and that believing ye might have life through his name.

— John 20:24–31.

EASTER

A LMIGHTY AND EVERLIVING GOD, give us today the great gladness of Christians that thou hast raised our Lord Jesus Christ from the dead, that through him all our failures, and all bodily death, are conquered for us. Keep us evermore from all fear that thou hast left us to the death we draw upon ourselves. In daring faith in the Easter promise, help us to commit ourselves again to obedience to thee. Make our hearts sure, by this Easter sign, that thou dost indeed perform thy will, and that in thy will is our life. Through Jesus Christ, our risen Lord.

Amen.

GRACES FOR MEALTIME

BLESS THE LORD, O my soul: and all that is within me, bless his holy name. Bless the Lord, O my soul, and forget not all his benefits: who forgiveth all thine iniquities; who healeth all thy diseases; who redeemeth thy life from destruction; who crowneth thee with lovingkindness and tender mercies; who satisfieth thy mouth with good things; so that thy youth is renewed like the eagle's. . . . Bless the Lord, O my soul."

In our eating and drinking, in our coming in and going out, in our living and dying, let everything be to thy glory, Lord. Amen.

All things come from thee, O Lord. Grant that we may use all things according to thy purpose. Amen.

Lord, all we have is thy free gift: forgive our undeserving: grant that we may give to thee our hearts and lives. Amen.